The Divine Cupcake Cookbook

50 Irresistible Recipes That Will Make You Go *YUMMMM...*

Disclaimer

No part of this eBook can be transmitted or reproduced in any form including print, electronic, photocopying, scanning, mechanical or recording without prior written permission from the author.

While the author has taken utmost efforts to ensure the accuracy of the written content, all readers are advised to follow information mentioned herein at their own risk. The author cannot be held responsible for any personal or commercial damage caused by misinterpretation of information. All readers are encouraged to seek professional advice when needed.

What You Will Find In This Cookbook?

Breakfast, snack time, high tea, desert after meal or the arrival of unexpected guests, Cupcakes are the perfect snack for every time.

This book contains 50 recipes for making a diverse variety of cupcakes. Starting from the basic cupcake recipe to colorful and delicious frosted cupcakes, this book has a cupcake recipe for all age groups and occasions.

And the best part is that the ingredients required to bake cupcakes are very common and most of them are always available in a standard kitchen pantry. Just a slight variation in the input and procedure, and you can make loads of different cupcakes at the same time.

This book contains the following stuff.

1. 50 recipes of cupcakes with nutritional facts.
2. Recipes of fruit cupcakes, cream frostings, diabetic cupcakes and low fat cupcakes.
3. Cupcakes for all age groups and preferences for example mom's favorite pumpkin cupcakes, vegan cupcakes and much more.

Some of the cupcake recipes presented in this book are:

1. Choco Mousse Cupcakes
2. Lemon Flavored Yoghurt Cupcakes
3. Cheesilicious Cupcakes
4. Scented Cupcakes
5. Drunken Cupcakes with Butter Rum Frosting
6. Divine Malt Cupcakes

Try out a few and keep your kitchen stocked with colorful yummilicious cupcakes.

Contents

Disclaimer 2
What You Will Find In This Cookbook? 3
Basic Rule of Thumb 13
Plain Egg Cupcakes 14
    Serving Size 14
    Nutritional Facts (Values per Cupcake) 14
    Ingredients 14
    Preparation Method 14
Quick Vanilla Cupcakes 16
    Serving Size 16
    Nutritional Facts (Values per Cupcake) 16
    Ingredients 16
    Preparation Method 16
Creamy Lemon Cupcakes 18
    Serving Size 18
    Nutritional Facts (Values per Cupcake) 18
    Ingredients 18
    Preparation Method 18
Coffee 'n' Cheese Cupcakes 19
    Serving Size 19
    Nutritional Facts (Values per Cupcake) 19
    Ingredients for Cupcakes 19
    Ingredients for Cheese Filling 19
    Ingredients for Coffee Filling 19
    Ingredients for Cream Cheese Frosting 19
    Preparation Method 20
Classic Homemade Vanilla Cupcake 22
    Serving Size 22
    Nutritional Facts (Values per Cupcake) 22
    Ingredients 22
    Preparation Method 22
Choco Fudge Cupcakes 24
    Serving Size 24

- Nutritional Facts (Values per Cupcake) 24
- Ingredients 24
- Preparation Method 24

Chocolicious Cupcakes 26
- Serving Size 26
- Nutritional Facts (Values per Cupcake) 26
- Ingredients 26
- Preparation Method 26

Light Pecan Cupcakes 28
- Serving Size 28
- Nutritional Facts (Values per Cupcake) 28
- Ingredients 28
- Preparation Method 28

Buttercream Vanilla Cupcakes 29
- Serving Size 29
- Nutritional Facts (Values per Cupcake) 29
- Ingredients for Cupcakes 29
- Ingredients for Buttercream Icing 29
- Preparation Method 29

Granny's Apple Cupcakes 31
- Serving Size 31
- Nutritional Facts (Values per Cupcake) 31
- Ingredients 31
- Preparation Method 31

Blue Velvet Cupcakes 33
- Serving Size 33
- Nutritional Facts (Values per Cupcake) 33
- Ingredients 33
- Ingredients for Frosting 33
- Preparation Method 34

Vegan Cupcakes 35
- Serving Size 35
- Nutritional Facts (Values per Cupcake) 35
- Ingredients 35

  Preparation Method 35

 Coconut Cupcakes with Cream Cheese Topping 37

  Serving Size 37

  Nutritional Facts (Values per Cupcake) 37

  Ingredients for Cupcakes 37

  Ingredients for Frosting 37

  Preparation Method 38

 Irish Guinness Cupcakes 39

  Serving Size 39

  Nutritional Facts (Values per Cupcake) 39

  Ingredients for Cupcakes 39

  Ingredients for Frosting 39

  Preparation Method 40

 Mom's Favorite Pumpkin Cupcakes 41

  Serving Size 41

  Nutritional Facts (Values per Cupcake) 41

  Ingredients 41

  Preparation Method 41

 Choco Mousse Cupcakes 42

  Serving Size 42

  Nutritional Facts (Values per Cupcake) 42

  Ingredients for Cupcakes 42

  Ingredients for Mousse Topping 42

  Preparation Method 43

 Strawberry Lovers 44

  Serving Size 44

  Nutritional Facts (Values per Cupcake) 44

  Ingredients for Cupcakes 44

  Ingredients for Strawberry Frosting 44

  Preparation Method 45

 Carrot Cupcakes with Cream Cheese Frosting 47

  Serving Size 47

  Nutritional Facts (Values per Cupcake) 47

  Ingredients for Cupcakes 47

- Ingredients for Cream Cheese Frosting ... 47
- Preparation Method ... 48

Cola Cupcakes ... 49
- Serving Size ... 49
- Nutritional Facts (Values per Cupcake) ... 49
- Ingredients ... 49
- Preparation Method ... 49

Chocolate Heavens ... 51
- Serving Size ... 51
- Nutritional Facts (Values per Cupcake) ... 51
- Ingredients ... 51
- Preparation Method ... 51

Eggless Vanilla Cupcakes ... 53
- Serving Size ... 53
- Nutritional Facts (Values per Cupcake) ... 53
- Ingredients ... 53
- Preparation Method ... 53

Zucchini Cupcakes with Brown Butter Frosting ... 55
- Serving Size ... 55
- Nutritional Facts (Values per Cupcake) ... 55
- Ingredients for Cupcakes ... 55
- Ingredients for Brown Butter Frosting ... 55
- Preparation Method ... 56

Colorful Cupcakes ... 57
- Serving Size ... 57
- Nutritional Facts (Values per Cupcake) ... 57
- Ingredients ... 57
- Preparation Method ... 57

Lemon Flavored Yoghurt Cupcakes ... 59
- Serving Size ... 59
- Nutritional Facts (Values per Cupcake) ... 59
- Ingredients ... 59
- Preparation Method ... 59

Nutty German Cupcakes ... 61

    Serving Size 61
    Nutritional Facts (Values per Cupcake) 61
    Ingredients for Cupcake 61
    Ingredients for Coconut Filling 61
    Ingredients for Chocolate Icing 62
    Preparation Method 62
Cheesilicious Cupcakes 63
    Serving Size 63
    Nutritional Facts (Values per Cupcake) 63
    Ingredients 63
    Preparation Method 63
Scented Cupcakes 65
    Serving Size 65
    Nutritional Facts (Values per Cupcake) 65
    Ingredients for Cupcakes 65
    Ingredients for Scented ingredients 65
    Ingredients for Icing 65
    Preparation Method 66
Drunken Cupcakes with Butter Rum Frosting 67
    Serving Size 67
    Nutritional Facts (Values per Cupcake) 67
    Ingredients for Cupcakes 67
    Ingredients for Butter Rum Frosting 67
    Ingredients for Butter Rum Glaze 67
    Preparation Method 68
Diabetic Cupcakes 70
    Serving Size 70
    Nutritional Facts (Values per Cupcake) 70
    Ingredients 70
    Preparation Method 71
Choco Banana Cupcakes 72
    Serving Size 72
    Nutritional Facts (Values per Cupcake) 72
    Ingredients 72

- Preparation Method 73
- **Tequila Cupcakes** 74
  - Serving Size 74
  - Nutritional Facts (Values per Cupcake) 74
  - Ingredients for Cupcakes 74
  - Ingredients for Frosting 74
  - Preparation Method 75
- **Cookies 'n' Cream Cupcakes** 76
  - Serving Size 76
  - Nutritional Facts (Values per Cupcake) 76
  - Ingredients for Cupcakes 76
  - Ingredients for Oreo Frosting 76
  - Preparation Method 77
- **Blueberry Cupcakes** 79
  - Serving Size 79
  - Nutritional Facts (Values per Cupcake) 79
  - Ingredients 79
  - Preparation Method 79
- **Peanut Butter Treat** 81
  - Serving Size 81
  - Nutritional Facts (Values per Cupcake) 81
  - Ingredients 81
  - Preparation Method 81
- **Spicy Coconut Cupcakes with Orange Cheese Frosting** 83
  - Serving Size 83
  - Nutritional Facts (Values per Cupcake) 83
  - Ingredients for Cupcakes 83
  - Ingredients for Orange Cheese Frosting 84
  - Preparation Method 84
- **Brown Orange Cupcakes** 86
  - Serving Size 86
  - Nutritional Facts (Values per Cupcake) 86
  - Ingredients for Cupcakes 86
  - Ingredients for Frosting 86

Preparation Method 87

Coconut Cupcakes with Condensed Milk Frosting 88
- Serving Size 88
- Nutritional Facts (Values per Cupcake) 88
- Ingredients for Cupcakes 88
- Ingredients for Condensed Milk Frosting 88
- Preparation Method 89

Death by Chocolate Cupcakes 92
- Serving Size 92
- Nutritional Facts (Values per Cupcake) 92
- Ingredients 92
- Preparation Method 92

Berrylicious White Chocolate Cupcakes 94
- Serving Size 94
- Nutritional Facts (Values per Cupcake) 94
- Ingredients 94
- Preparation Method 94

Mocha Cupcakes 96
- Serving Size 96
- Nutritional Facts (Values per Cupcake) 96
- Ingredients for Cupcakes 96
- Ingredients for Mocha Frosting 96
- Preparation Method 97

Celebration Cupcakes 99
- Serving Size 99
- Nutritional Facts (Values per Cupcake) 99
- Ingredients for Cupcakes 99
- Ingredients for Frosting 99
- Preparation Method 99

Strawberry Marmalade Cupcakes 101
- Serving Size 101
- Nutritional Facts (Values per Cupcake) 101
- Ingredients 101
- Preparation Method 101

- German Peppermint Cupcakes 103
  - Serving Size 103
  - Nutritional Facts (Values per Cupcake) 103
  - Ingredients for Cupcakes 103
  - Ingredients for Frosting 103
  - Preparation Method 104
- Mayonnaise in a Cupcake 105
  - Serving Size 105
  - Nutritional Facts (Values per Cupcake) 105
  - Ingredients 105
  - Preparation Method 105
- Boston Cream Surprise Cupcakes 107
  - Serving Size 107
  - Nutritional Facts (Values per Cupcake) 107
  - Ingredients for cupcakes 107
  - Ingredients for Cream Filling 107
  - Ingredients for Chocolate glaze 108
  - Preparation Method 108
- Sweet Bacon Cupcakes 110
  - Serving Size 110
  - Nutritional Facts (Values per Cupcake) 110
  - Ingredients for Cupcakes 110
  - Ingredients for Maple Frosting 110
  - Preparation Method 111
- Divine Malt Cupcakes 112
  - Serving Size 112
  - Nutritional Facts (Values per Cupcake) 112
  - Ingredients for Cupcakes 112
  - Ingredients for Buttercream Frosting 112
  - Preparation Method 113
- Classic Sweet Potato Muffins 115
  - Serving Size 115
  - Nutritional Facts (Values per Cupcake) 115
  - Ingredients 115

    Preparation Method 115
Simple Champagne Cupcakes 117
    Serving Size 117
    Nutritional Facts (Values per Cupcake) 117
    Ingredients 117
    Preparation Method 117
Pineapple 'n' Coconut Cupcake 119
    Serving Size 119
    Nutritional Facts (Values per Cupcake) 119
    Ingredients 119
    Preparation Method 119

Basic Rule of Thumb

Before you start following any of the recipes, you need to know one basic thing about baking, especially if you are baking for the first time.

The recipes contained within this book are very easy. You just need to follow the basic rule of thumb of baking while making any of these cupcakes, and that is use the exact quantity of basic ingredients (eggs, butter, oil baking soda, baking powder and flour).

While you can slightly increase or decrease additional ingredients such as sugar, cocoa powder, nuts etcetera but changing the amount of basic ingredients with proportion to the serving size may affect the final outcome.

So if you are doubling the serving size, make sure you double the quantity of basic ingredients precisely.

Plain Egg Cupcakes

Serving Size

Makes 12 cupcakes

Nutritional Facts (Values per Cupcake)

Calories/Cupcake: 161.8

Protein: 2.2 g

Total Fat: 8.5 g

Cholesterol: 51.3 mg

Total Carbohydrate: 19.2 g

Ingredients

Butter – half cup

Eggs – 2

Sugar – 2/3 cup

Salt – ½ tsp

Flour – 1 cup

Vanilla Extract – 1 tsp

Baking powder – 1 tsp

Preparation Method

7. Set the oven to preheat at 350°F.
8. Line a cupcake baking pan.
9. In a large bowl, combine all the ingredients.
10. Using an electric beater beat the ingredients till it becomes a smooth batter.
11. Pour the batter into the lined cups. Make sure you just fill half of the cups.
12. Put the pan in the preheated oven for 18 – 20 minutes.

13. To check whether it is fully baked, insert a toothpick in any of the cupcake. If it comes out clean, it means it is baked. If there are any cake chunks on the toothpick, it implies the cupcakes need to be baked for a few more minutes.

The basic plain cupcakes are ready to devour. You can serve them as is or decorate them with any frosting you want.

Quick Vanilla Cupcakes

Serving Size

    Makes 12 cupcakes

Nutritional Facts (Values per Cupcake)

    Calories/Cupcake: 182

    Protein: 2.4 g

    Total Fat: 6.7 g

    Cholesterol: 22 mg

    Total Carbohydrate: 28 g

Ingredients

    Milk – ½ cup

    Sugar – 1 cup

    Soft shortening – 1/3 cup

    Egg – 1

    All purpose flour – 1 1/3 cups

    Salt – ½ tsp

    Baking powder – ½ Tbsp

    Vanilla essence – 1 ½ tsp

    Cream – 1 Tbsp (Optional)

Preparation Method

1. Set the oven to preheat at 350°F.
2. Combine sugar, flour, salt and baking powder in a large bowl. Mix well.
3. Add in it, the shortening, milk, eggs and vanilla extract. Beat using an electric beater, till it becomes a thick and smooth batter. You can also add cream to make it thicker.
4. Line a regular muffin baking pan.

5. Half fill the muffin cups with the batter.

6. Put it in the preheated oven for 20 – 22 minutes or until a toothpick when inserted in it comes out clean.

Serve it as it or top it up with vanilla frosting. (If you intend to do the frosting, then let the cupcakes cool off for a bit frosting them up)

Creamy Lemon Cupcakes

Serving Size

Makes 24 cupcakes

Nutritional Facts (Values per Cupcake)

Calories/Cupcake: 210

Protein: 2.2 g

Total Fat: 8.6 g

Cholesterol: 32.3 mg

Total Carbohydrate: 31.5 g

Ingredients

White cake mix – 18 oz.

Eggs – 3

Frozen lemonade concentrate, defrosted – 6 oz. (less 2 Tbsp)

Sour cream – 8 oz.

Cream cheese frosting, whipped – 12 oz.

Soft cream cheese – 3 oz.

Preparation Method

1. Set the oven to preheat at 350°F.
2. In a large bowl, add cake mix, cream cheese, sour cream, lemon concentrate and eggs. Beat till it becomes a smooth batter.
3. Line a cupcake baking pan with cupcake paper.
4. Fill ¾ of the paper-lined cups with the batter.
5. Put the pan in the preheated oven for 20 minutes or until a toothpick comes out clean.
6. Set aside to cool for a while.
7. Top up the cakes with whipped cream cheese frosting.

Coffee 'n' Cheese Cupcakes

Serving Size

    Makes 24 cupcakes

Nutritional Facts (Values per Cupcake)

    Calories/Cupcake: 261.5

    Protein: 2.6 g

    Total Fat: 13.3 g

    Cholesterol: 44.9 mg

    Total Carbohydrate: 32.7 g

Ingredients for Cupcakes

    Cupcakes

    Eggs – 3

    Water – 1 ¼ cups

    White cake mix – 18 oz.

    Oil – 1/3 cup

Ingredients for Cheese Filling

    Kahlua – 3 Tbsp

    Mascarpone cheese – 8 oz.

    French vanilla cool whip – 8 oz.

    Sweetened condensed milk – ¼ cup

Ingredients for Coffee Filling

    Icing sugar – half cup

    Water – 2/3 cup

    Instant coffee – 4 ½ tsp

Ingredients for Cream Cheese Frosting

Icing sugar – 2 cups

Soft cream cheese – 8 oz.

Vanilla essence – 1 tsp

Soft butter – half cup

Chocolate sprinkles/finely grated chocolate to garnish

Preparation Method

To make the cheese filling,

1. In a large bowl, add mascarpone cheese, condensed milk and Kahlua. Beat well till it becomes smooth.
2. Fold the cool whip in it.
3. Put in the refrigerator for at least 4 hours or maximum overnight.
4. When there is half hour left in taking out the cheese filling, make the cupcake batter as directed on the cake mix box.
5. Pour the batter in paper lined muffin tray and put in the oven to make.

While the cupcakes are in the oven, make the coffee filling.

6. Boil water in a microwave or saucepan.
7. Add instant coffee in the boiling water and stir till the coffee is completely dissolved.
8. Stir in icing sugar and set aside to cool for a while.
9. When the cupcakes are fully baked, make a few holes in each of them, using a toothpick or fork. (Do not make so many holes or the cake will break. Three fork piercings are more than enough).
10. When the coffee is cooled, use silicon baking brush to brush the coffee over the cupcakes.
11. Next, fill an icing bag with the chilled cheese filling.
12. Pipe out about a spoonful filling on top of each cupcake.

To make the cream cheese frosting,

13. In a large bowl, beat cream cheese and butter on low speed till it becomes a smooth creamy blend.

14. Start adding the icing slowly gradually while beating constantly.

15. Finally, add the vanilla essence while increasing the speed of the beater to medium.

16. Keep blend till it becomes fluffy.

17. Spread the frosting on each cupcake.

18. Garnish it with chocolate sprinkles or grated chocolate.

Classic Homemade Vanilla Cupcake

Serving Size

Makes 24 cupcakes

Nutritional Facts (Values per Cupcake)

Calories/Cupcake: 247

Protein: 2.4 g

Total Fat: 7.1 g

Cholesterol: 33.4 mg

Total Carbohydrate: 44.2 g

Ingredients

Milk – half cup

Unsalted butter – 3 oz.

All purpose flour – 1 ¼ cups

Vanilla essence – 1 tsp

Granulated sugar – 1 cup

Baking powder – 1 ¼ tsp

Egg – 1

Salt – ¼ tsp

Frosting

Half-and-half – 2 Tbsp

Icing sugar – 1 ½ cups

Vanilla essence – 1 tsp

Preparation Method

1. Set the oven to preheat at 375°F.
2. Line a cupcake baking pan with cupcake paper liners.

3. Beat cream and granulated sugar in a large bowl.

4. Add in it, egg, salt, vanilla essence and baking powder. Beat well.

5. Add a spoon of flour while beating constantly. Next, add a spoon of milk and then again a flour of spoon. Keep doing so till you add all the flour and milk. Make sure you are beating constantly while adding milk and flour. Keep beating till it becomes smooth.

6. Fill half of the paper lined cups with this batter.

7. Put the pan in the preheated oven for 18 – 20 minutes or until a toothpick when inserted in it comes out clean.

8. When the cupcakes are cooked through, set them aside to cool down for at least 40 minutes.

9. To make the frosting, combine icing sugar, vanilla essence and half-and-half. Whip till it become a soft and fluffy paste.

10. Spread a spoonful frosting on each cupcake.

Choco Fudge Cupcakes

Serving Size

    Makes 12 cupcakes

Nutritional Facts (Values per Cupcake)

    Calories/Cupcake: 282.4

    Protein: 4 g

    Total Fat: 11.8 g

    Cholesterol: 18.3 mg

    Total Carbohydrate: 43.2 g

Ingredients

    Brown sugar – 1 cup

    Half-and-half – 1 cup

    Baking cocoa, unsweetened – ¼ cup

    Canola Oil – 1/3 cup

    Baking powder – 1 tsp

    Semisweet chocolate chips – 1 cup

    All purpose flour – 1 ¾ cups

    Baking soda – 1 tsp

    Pinch of Cinnamon

    Egg – 1

    Vanilla extract – 1 tsp

    Chopped walnuts – half cup

    Salt – ½ tsp

Preparation Method

1. Set the oven to preheat at 350°F.

2. Line a cupcake baking pan with paper liners.

3. In a bowl, combine brown sugar, baking cocoa, salt, baking powder, flour, baking soda and cinnamon. Mix well.

4. In another small bowl, beat the egg slightly. Add in it, milk, oil and vanilla extract.

5. Fold this liquid mixture in the flour mixture.

6. Stir in the chocolate chips and chopped walnuts.

7. Half fill the cups of the baking pan with this batter.

8. Put the pan in the preheated oven for 22 – 25 minutes or until a toothpick when inserted in it comes out clean.

9. Serve as it is or top it up with chocolate syrup.

Chocolicious Cupcakes

Serving Size

Makes 16 cupcakes

Nutritional Facts (Values per Cupcake)

Calories/Cupcake: 156

Protein: 1.5 g

Total Fat: 7.1 g

Cholesterol: 0.0 mg

Total Carbohydrate: 22.5 g

Ingredients

Cocoa powder – 1/3 cup

Flour – 1 ½ cups

Oil – half cup

Vinegar – 1 tsp

Granulated sugar – 1 cup

Water – 1 cup

Baking soda – 1 tsp

Vanilla extract – 1 tsp

Salt – 1 tsp

Preparation Method

1. Set the oven to preheat at 350°F.
2. Line a muffin tray with paper liners.
3. In a large bowl, add all the ingredients.
4. With an electric beater, beat all the ingredients till it becomes a smooth batter.

5. Spoon out the batter into the paper lined muffin tray. Fill ¾ of the each muffin cup.

6. Put the pan in the preheated oven for 20 – 25 minutes or until a toothpick when inserted in it comes out clean.

Light Pecan Cupcakes

Serving Size

Makes 24 cupcakes

Nutritional Facts (Values per Cupcake)

Calories/Cupcake: 127

Protein: 1.2 g

Total Fat: 8.8 g

Cholesterol: 29.1 mg

Total Carbohydrate: 11.6 g

Ingredients

Eggs – 2

All purpose flour – half cup

Butter, melted – 2/3

Pecans, chopped – 1 cup

Brown sugar – 1 cup

Cooking spray

Preparation Method

1. Set the oven to preheat at 350°F.
2. Grease a muffing baking pan with cooking spray.
3. In a large bowl, combine all the ingredients. Beat well to form a smooth batter.
4. Fill ¾ of each greased muffin cup with this batter.
5. Put the pan in the preheated oven for 18 – 20 minutes or until a toothpick when inserted in it comes out clean.

Buttercream Vanilla Cupcakes

Serving Size

Makes 16 cupcakes

Nutritional Facts (Values per Cupcake)

Calories/Cupcake: 227

Protein: 4.7 g

Total Fat: 25.2 g

Cholesterol: 110.7 mg

Total Carbohydrate: 102.2 g

Ingredients for Cupcakes

Milk – 1 cups

Sugar – 2 cups

Self rising flour – 1 ½ cups

Unsalted butter – 8 oz.

Eggs – 4

Vanilla essence – 1 tsp

All purpose flour – 1 ¼ cups

Ingredients for Buttercream Icing

Vanilla essence – 2 tsp

Icing sugar – 8 cups

Unsalted butter, softened – 8 0z.

Milk – half cup

Preparation Method

1. Set the oven to preheat at 350°F.
2. Line a regular cupcake baking pan with cupcake paper liners.

3. Combine the self rising flour and all purpose flour in a bowl. Set aside.

4. Put butter in another large bowl. Beat it using an electric beater on medium speed, till it becomes smooth like cream.

5. Start adding sugar in it gradually while beating constantly, till it becomes fluffy.

6. Start adding eggs in it. Add one egg at a time, beat it for a minute and then add another.

7. Add ¼ of the flour mixture while beating continuously. Then add ¼ of the milk, then again ¼ of the flour mixture and so on. In short, add flour mixture and milk alternatively in four parts, while running the electric beater continuously.

8. Finally add in the vanilla essence and beat till it becomes a smooth batter.

9. Pour out the batter in the lined baking pan while filling ¾ of every cupcake slot.

10. Put the pan in the preheated oven for 20 – 25 minutes or until a toothpick when inserted in the middle of a cupcake comes out clean.

11. Set aside to cool for 10 minutes.

To prepare the buttercream icing,

12. Combine soft butter, half of the icing sugar, milk and vanilla essence in a large bowl.

13. Beat till it becomes smooth and fluffy.

14. Start adding the remaining sugar. Add 1 cup at a time while beating constantly. If you want, you can also add a few drops of any food color in it.

15. Spoon out the icing on top of each cupcake and serve!

Granny's Apple Cupcakes

Serving Size

Makes 24 cupcakes

Nutritional Facts (Values per Cupcake)

Calories/Cupcake: 206

Protein: 2.1 g

Total Fat: 7.9 g

Cholesterol: 20.3 mg

Total Carbohydrate: 32.3 g

Ingredients

Sugar – 2 cups

Baking soda – 2 tsp

Water – 2 cups

Ground cloves – ½ tsp

Butter – 8 oz.

Ground nutmeg – 2 tsp

Apples – 6 large

Flour – 3 ½ cups

Cinnamon powder – 2 tsp

Preparation Method

1. Set the oven to preheat at 350°F.
2. Line the cupcake baking tray with paper liners.
3. Grate the apples without removing its skin.
4. In a large saucepan, add the grated apples, water, sugar, cinnamon powder, butter, ground nutmeg and ground cloves. Bring it to a boil.

5. Set aside to cool it off.
6. Add in the saucepan, baking soda and flour. Mix well.
7. Fill ¾ of each paper lined cupcake with this batter.
8. Put the pan in the preheated oven for 20 – 25 minutes or until a toothpick when inserted in it comes out clean.

Blue Velvet Cupcakes

Serving Size

Makes 24 cupcakes

Nutritional Facts (Values per Cupcake)

Calories/Cupcake: 237

Protein: 2.9 g

Total Fat: 11.5 g

Cholesterol: 46.6 mg

Total Carbohydrate: 31.1 g

Ingredients

Cocoa powder – 2 Tbsp

All purpose flour, sifted – 2 ½ cups

Sugar – 1 ½ cup

White vinegar – 1 tsp

Eggs -2

Buttermilk – 1 cup

Soft unsalted butter – half cup

Water – 2 oz.

Baking soda – 1 tsp

Blue food coloring – 2 oz.

Vanilla essence – 1 tsp

Salt – 1 tsp

Ingredients for Frosting

Soft unsalted butter – half cup

Vanilla essence – 1 tsp

Cream cheese, softened – 8 oz.

Icing sugar – 1 ½ cup

Preparation Method

1. Set the oven to preheat at 350°F.
2. Line a cupcake baking tray with paper liners.
3. In a small bowl, combine cocoa powder and blue food color. Set aside.
4. In another small bowl, mix vinegar and baking soda. Set aside.
5. In a large bowl, add butter and sugar. Beat till it becomes smooth and fluffy.
6. Add eggs in and beat for another few minutes.
7. Fold the cocoa-food color mixture in it.
8. Now add flour and salt in it. Mix well.
9. Add buttermilk, beat for about a minute.
10. Add vanilla extract and beat for another minute.
11. Finally, add water and beat for one more minute. That's it. Now turn off the beater.
12. Fold the vinegar-baking soda paste in it. Do not beat after adding it.
13. Spoon out the batter in the paper lined cupcake cups.
14. Put the pan in the preheated oven for 17 – 20 minutes or until the cake springs back when lightly touched in the center.
15. Set aside to cool for 10 minute.
16. Meanwhile, blend together all the frosting ingredients. Blend till it becomes fluffy.
17. Spoon out the frosting on the cupcakes and serve!

Vegan Cupcakes

Serving Size

Makes 24 cupcakes

Nutritional Facts (Values per Cupcake)

Calories/Cupcake: 105

Protein: 1.5 g

Total Fat: 2.4 g

Cholesterol: 0.0 mg

Total Carbohydrate: 19.6 g

Ingredients

Sugar – ¾ cup

Baking powder – 1 ½ tsp

Baking soda – 2 tsp

Grated carrots, grated – 2 cups

Cinnamon powder – 1 ½ tsp

Coconut flakes – 1 cup

Ground Nutmeg – ½ tsp

Applesauce, unsweetened – half cup

Canola oil – ¼ cup

Flour – 2 ½ cups

Crushed pineapple – 1 cup

Salt – ½ tsp

Preparation Method

1. Set the oven to preheat at 325°F.
2. Line a cupcake baking pan with paper liners.

3. Combine baking powder and applesauce in a small bowl. Mix till it becomes a foamy paste. Set aside.

4. In another large bowl, add sugar, cinnamon powder, flour, baking soda, salt and ground nutmeg. Mix well.

5. Add in the crushed pineapples, grated carrots and applesauce paste. Mix well.

6. Finally, stir in coconut flakes.

7. Pour the batter in the paper-lined cupcake pan. Fill ¾ of each cupcake slot.

8. Put the pan in the preheated oven for 25 – 30 minutes or until a toothpick when inserted in it comes out clean.

Coconut Cupcakes with Cream Cheese Topping

Serving Size

Makes 12 cupcakes

Nutritional Facts (Values per Cupcake)

Calories/Cupcake: 588

Protein: 5.1 g

Total Fat: 33.4 g

Cholesterol: 62.4 mg

Total Carbohydrate: 69.4 g

Ingredients for Cupcakes

Egg whites – 3

Sugar – ¾ cup

Coconut milk – ¾ cup (substitute: whole milk)

Sweetened coconut flakes – 1 cup

Baking powder – 2 tsp

Unsalted butter – half cup

All purpose flour – 1 ¾ cups

Almond essence – ½

Salt – ½ tsp

Vanilla essence – 1 tsp

Ingredients for Frosting

White chocolate, melted – 2 oz.

Icing sugar – 2 cups

Cream cheese – 8 oz.

Juice of half lime

Unsalted butter – half cup

Sweetened coconut flakes – 1 ½ cup (for garnishing)

Preparation Method

1. Set the oven to preheat at 350°F.
2. Line a regular muffin baking tray with paper liners.
3. In a bowl, sift baking powder, flour and salt. Set aside.
4. In another bowl, put egg whites, vanilla essence, almond essence and coconut milk. Set aside.
5. In another large bowl, beat butter and sugar for about 4 minute or till the color of butter lightens.
6. Start adding the flour mixture and the egg white mixture gradually and alternatively, while beating continuously. Make sure you start with dry mixture and ends on the same.
7. Fold coconut flakes in it.
8. Scoop out this batter in the paper lined muffin cups, while filling ¾ of each cup.
9. Put the pan in the preheated oven for 25 – 30 minutes or until a toothpick when inserted in the center of a cupcake comes out clean.
10. Set aside to cool for 10 minutes.
11. Meanwhile, beat butter and cream cheese in a large bowl. Keep blending till it becomes smooth.
12. Add lime juice and melted white chocolate in it. Blend well.
13. Finally, add icing sugar in it. Beat till it becomes gooey smooth.
14. Spoon out about 3 tablespoons frosting on each cupcake.
15. Garnish with coconut flakes and serve.

Irish Guinness Cupcakes

Serving Size

Makes 12 cupcakes

Nutritional Facts (Values per Cupcake)

Calories/Cupcake: 357

Protein: 2.8 g

Total Fat: 13.3 g

Cholesterol: 48.5 mg

Total Carbohydrate: 51 g

Ingredients for Cupcakes

Dutch processed cocoa powder, sifted – 1/3 cup

Egg – 1

Unsalted butter – half cup

Brown sugar – half cup

Baking soda – ½ tsp

All purpose flour, sifted – 1 cup

Sour cream – ¼ cup

White sugar – half cup

Guinness stout – half cup

Salt – ½ tsp

Ingredients for Frosting

Milk – ½ Tbsp

Unsalted butter – ¼ cup

Icing sugar – 2 cups

Irish cream – 1 ½ Tbsp

Green sprinkles for garnishing

Preparation Method

1. Set the oven to preheat at 350°F.
2. Line a cupcake baking pan with paper liners.
3. Melt butter in a saucepan. Add in it, brown sugar, Guinness stout and cocoa powder. Keep whisking it till it becomes a smooth mixture.
4. Remove the saucepan off heat and set aside to cool.
5. In a large bowl, add flour, salt, white sugar and baking soda. Mix well.
6. Add in the same bowl, the Guinness mixture. Beat for a minute using an electric beater on medium speed.
7. Finally add eggs and sour cream in it and beat for 2 more minutes or until it becomes smooth.
8. Fill ¾ of the paper-lined cupcake cups with this batter.
9. Put the pan in the preheated oven for 20 – 25 minutes or until a toothpick when inserted in it comes out clean.
10. Set aside to cool for 15 minutes.
11. Meanwhile, beat butter in a large bowl till it becomes fluffy.
12. Add salt in it while beating continuously.
13. Reduce the speed of the beater to low and then start adding sugar gradually. Add one spoon at a time while beating continuously.
14. Once you have thoroughly beaten in all the sugar, add Irish cream and milk. Beat till it becomes smooth and fluffy.
15. Spoon it over the cupcakes.
16. Top it up with green sprinkles and serve.

Mom's Favorite Pumpkin Cupcakes

Serving Size

Makes 24 cupcakes

Nutritional Facts (Values per Cupcake)

Calories/Cupcake: 115

Protein: 1.7 g

Total Fat: 6 g

Cholesterol: 23.2 mg

Total Carbohydrate: 13.9 g

Ingredients

Eggs – 3

Canned Pumpkin – 15 oz.

Vegetable oil – 1/3 cup

Spice cake mix – 1

Water – 1/3 cup

Preparation Method

1. Set the oven to preheat at 350°F.
2. Line a regular cupcake baking pan with paper liners.
3. In a large bowl, mix all the ingredients. Beat for 2 minutes, with an electric beater on medium heat.
4. Fill ¾ of every paper-lined cupcake cup with this batter.
5. Put it in the preheated oven for 20 minutes or until a toothpick when inserted in it comes out clean.

Choco Mousse Cupcakes

Serving Size

Makes 12 cupcakes

Nutritional Facts (Values per Cupcake)

Calories/Cupcake: 323

Protein: 5.7 g

Total Fat: 16 g

Cholesterol: 0.4 mg

Total Carbohydrate: 44.5 g

Ingredients for Cupcakes

All purpose flour – 1 cup

Soymilk – 1 cup

Canola oil – 1/3 cup

Baking powder – ½ tsp

Sugar – ¾ cup

Cocoa powder – 1/3 cup

Apple cider vinegar – 1 tsp

Baking soda – ¾ tsp

Salt – ¼ tsp

Vanilla essence – 2 tsp

Ingredients for Mousse Topping

Soymilk – ¼ cup

Semi sweet chocolate chips, melted – 12 oz.

Vanilla essence – 1 tsp

Silken tofu, extra firm – 12.3 oz

Maple syrup – 2 tsp

Preparation Method

1. Set the oven to preheat at 350°F.

2. Line a cupcake baking pan with paper liners.

3. In a bowl, combine apple cider vinegar and soy milk. Whisk it for a few minutes. Let it sit for a while till it starts to curdle.

4. Now add oil, sugar and vanilla essence in it. Beat till it becomes frothy.

5. In another bowl, combine baking powder, flour, salt, baking soda and cocoa powder. Mix well.

6. Fold this dry ingredient mixture in the soy milk mixture. Keep folding it till are no lumps remain in it.

7. Spoon out the batter in the paper-lined cups. Fill ¾ of every cupcake slot.

8. Put the pan in the preheated oven for 18 – 20 minutes or until a toothpick when inserted in it comes out clean.

9. Set it aside to cool.

10. Meanwhile, let's make the mousse topping.

11. In a blender, add soy milk, vanilla essence, tofu and maple syrup. Blend till it becomes a smooth puree.

12. Add the melted chocolate in it and blend again for 2 – 3 minutes.

13. Pour out this puree in a container. Cover the container with a lid or plastic wrap and put it in the refrigerator for at least an hour.

14. Fill the mousse topping in a large pastry bag.

15. Pipe it out on each cupcake.

Strawberry Lovers

Serving Size

Makes 12 cupcakes

Nutritional Facts (Values per Cupcake)

Calories/Cupcake: 477

Protein: 3.2 g

Total Fat: 23.7 g

Cholesterol: 77.2 mg

Total Carbohydrate: 64.8 g

Ingredients for Cupcakes

All purpose flour – 1 ½ cups

Fresh strawberries, sliced in half – 1 cup

Unsalted butter – 4 oz.

Baking powder – 1 tsp

Egg whites – 2

Sugar – 1 cup

Salt – ¼ tsp

Vanilla extract – 1 tsp

Milk – ¼ cup

Egg – 1

Ingredients for Strawberry Frosting

Strawberry puree – 3 Tbsp

Vanilla extract – ½ tsp

Unsalted butter – 8 oz.

Pinch of salt

Icing sugar – 3 ½ cups

Fresh strawberries to garnish

Preparation Method

1. Set the oven to preheat at 350°F.
2. Line a cupcake baking pan with paper liners.
3. Put the fresh strawberries in an electric blender. Blend it well to form a puree.
4. Take the strawberry puree out in a large bowl and mix milk in it. Set aside.
5. In a bowl, put baking powder, flour and salt. Mix well and set aside.
6. In another large bowl, beat butter using an electric beater on medium speed. Beat till it becomes fluffy.
7. Reduce the speed of the beater to medium and then start adding sugar in it. Add sugar gradually while beating constantly.
8. When all the sugar is thoroughly blended, slowly add egg and then egg whites. Beat till it becomes a smooth batter.
9. Finally, beat in vanilla extract.
10. Add ¼ of the flour mixture while beating continuously. Then add ¼ of the strawberry puree-milk mixture, then again ¼ of the flour mixture and so on. In short, add flour mixture and strawberry puree-milk mixture alternatively in four parts, while running the electric beater continuously.
11. Fill ¾ of each paper-lined cupcake cup with this batter.
12. Put the pan in the preheated oven for 20 – 25 minutes or until they pick up a light brown color.
13. Set aside to cool.

Meanwhile, prepare the strawberry frosting.

14. Beat butter and salt in a bowl, using an electric beater on medium speed. Beat till it becomes fluffy.
15. Lower down the speed to slow and add icing sugar in it. Beat well.
16. Finally, add vanilla extract and strawberry puree. Blend well.
17. Spread this frosting on top of each cupcake.

18. Garnish each cupcake with a fresh strawberry and serve.

Carrot Cupcakes with Cream Cheese Frosting

Serving Size

Makes 22 – 24 cupcakes

Nutritional Facts (Values per Cupcake)

Calories/Cupcake: 510.5

Protein: 4.5 g

Total Fat: 31.4 g

Cholesterol: 72.6 mg

Total Carbohydrate: 55.4 g

Ingredients for Cupcakes

All purpose flour, sifted – 2 cups

Grated carrots – 3 cups

Sugar – 2 cups

Large eggs – 3

Chopped walnuts – 1 cup

Ground cinnamon – 2 tsp

Raisins – 1 cup

Vanilla essence – 1 tsp

Baking soda – 2 tsp

Canola oil – 1 1/3 cups

Salt – 1 ½ tsp

Ingredients for Cream Cheese Frosting

Powdered sugar – 1 lb

Unsalted butter – 8 oz.

Cream cheese – 12 oz.

Vanilla essence — 1 tsp

Preparation Method

1. Set the oven to preheat at 350°F.
2. Line a muffin baking pan with paper liners.
3. In a bowl, add salt, flour, baking soda, and cinnamon. Mix well and set aside.
4. In a large bowl, put sugar, vanilla essence and oil. Beat well with an electric beater on low speed.
5. Start adding eggs in it. Add one egg at a time, while beating constantly.
6. Add half of the flour mixture in it while the beater is still running. Beat till the batter becomes smooth and then turn off the beater.
7. Now add the chopped walnuts, grated carrots and raisins in the remaining flour mixture. Mix well and fold it in the batter bowl.
8. Pour out the batter in the paper-lined muffin pan while filling ¾ of each muffin tin.
9. Put the muffin pan in the preheated oven. Increase the oven temperature to 400°F for 10 minutes.
10. After 10 minutes, lower the over temperature back to 350°F and bake for 30 – 35 more minutes or inserted in it comes out clean.
11. Place it on a rack to cool off for a while.
12. Meanwhile, prepare the frosting.
13. Beat the cream cheese, vanilla essence and butter in a large bowl.
14. Start adding sugar in it while beating constantly.
15. Keep on blending till it becomes smooth and fluffy.
16. Spread the frosting on each cupcake and serve.

Cola Cupcakes

Serving Size

Makes 24 cupcakes

Nutritional Facts (Values per Cupcake)

Calories/Cupcake: 158.5

Protein: 2.3 g

Total Fat: 5.3 g

Cholesterol: 15.9 mg

Total Carbohydrate: 25.7 g

Ingredients

All purpose flour – 1 ¾ cups

Canola oil – half cup

Baking soda – 2 tsp

Cola – 1 cup (substitute: strong coffee)

Cocoa powder, sifted – ¾ cup

Baking powder – 1 tsp

Sugar – 2 cups (substitute: brown sugar)

Buttermilk – 1 cup

Eggs – 2

Pinch of salt

Vanilla essence – 1 tsp

Preparation Method

1. Set the oven to preheat at 350°F.
2. Line a cupcake baking pan with paper liners.

3. In a bowl, combine flour, sugar, baking soda, baking powder, cocoa powder and salt. Mix well using a wire whisk.

4. Add eggs, cola, oil and vanilla essence in it. Mix well using a wire whisk or alternatively, beat for 2 minutes with an electric mixer on medium heat.

5. Fill the batter in the paper lined cups.

6. Put the pan in the preheated oven for 20 – 25 minutes or until a toothpick when inserted in it comes out clean.

Chocolate Heavens

Serving Size

Makes 12 cupcakes

Nutritional Facts (Values per Cupcake)

Calories/Cupcake: 292

Protein: 3.6 g

Total Fat: 16.1g

Cholesterol: 77 mg

Total Carbohydrate: 37.3 g

Ingredients

Eggs – 3

Unsalted butter, melted – ¾ cup

All purpose flour – ¾ cup

White sugar – 2/3 cup

Baking powder – 1 tsp

Brown sugar – 2/3 cup

Unsweetened cocoa powder – half cup

Almond extract – ½ tsp

Vanilla extract – ½ tsp

Semi sweet chocolate chips – 2/3 cup

Salt – ¼ tsp

Preparation Method

1. Set the oven to preheat at 325°F.
2. Line a cupcake baking pan with paper liners.

3. Combine cocoa powder, salt, baking powder and flour in a bowl. Mix well and set aside.

4. In another bowl, add butter, white sugar and brown sugar. Beat till it becomes smooth.

5. Add in it, almond and vanilla extract while beating constantly.

6. Start adding eggs in it. Add one egg at a time while beating continuously.

7. Finally, add the flour mixture in it and beat well till all the ingredients are thoroughly mixed.

8. Finally, add chocolate chips in it and stir.

9. Pour out the batter in the paper-lined cupcake pan while filling ¾ of each cupcake tin.

10. Put the pan in the preheated oven for 25 – 30 minutes or until a toothpick when inserted in it comes out with a bit of melted chocolate on it.

11. Let it cool for a while and serve.

Eggless Vanilla Cupcakes

Serving Size

Makes 12 cupcakes

Nutritional Facts (Values per Cupcake)

Calories/Cupcake: 182

Protein: 2.1 g

Total Fat: 8.0 g

Cholesterol: 0.0 mg

Total Carbohydrate: 25.1 g

Ingredients

Apple cider vinegar – 1 tsp

Soymilk – 1 cup

Vanilla extract – 2 tsp

Baking powder – ¾ tsp

Canola oil – 1/3 cup

Cornstarch – 2 tbsp

Sugar – ¾ cup

Baking soda – ½ tsp

Almond extract – ½ tsp

All purpose flour, sifted – 1 ¼ cups

Salt – ¼ tsp

Preparation Method

1. Set the oven to preheat at 350°F.
2. Line a muffin baking pan with paper liners.

3. In a large bowl, whisk apple cider vinegar and soy milk. Let it sit for a while until it is curdled.

4. When the soy milk mixture is curdled, add in it oil, vanilla extract, sugar and almond extract. Beat well till all the ingredients are well combined.

5. Add in it the cornstarch, flour, baking soda, salt and baking powder. Mix till all the lumps are dissolved and well combined.

6. Spoon out the batter in the paper-lined muffin pan while filling ¾ of each muffin tin.

7. Put the pan in the preheated oven for 20 – 22 minutes.

8. Let it cool completely before serving.

Zucchini Cupcakes with Brown Butter Frosting

Serving Size

Makes 20 cupcakes

Nutritional Facts (Values per Cupcake)

Calories/Cupcake: 293

Protein: 2.8 g

Total Fat: 11 g

Cholesterol: 40.5 mg

Total Carbohydrate: 46.5 g

Ingredients for Cupcakes

Shredded zucchini – 1 ½ cups

Eggs – 3

Baking soda – 1 tsp

Almond extract – 1 tsp

Vegetable oil – half cup

Sugar – 1 1/3 cups

Baking powder – 2 tsp

Ground cloves – ½ tsp

Orange juice – half cup

Cinnamon powder – 2 tsp

All purpose flour – 2 ½ cups

Salt – 1 tsp

Ingredients for Brown Butter Frosting

Margarine – half cup

Icing sugar – 2 cups

Milk — ¼ cup

Brown sugar — 1 cup

Vanilla extract — 1 tsp

Preparation Method

1. Set the oven to preheat at 350°F.
2. Line a cupcake baking pan with paper liners.
3. In a large bowl, combine sugar, eggs, orange juice, oil, cloves and almond extract. Beat till it becomes a smooth puree.
4. In another bowl, combine cinnamon powder, all purpose flour, baking powder, salt and baking soda. Mix well.
5. Fold this dry ingredient mixture in the egg mixture.
6. Stir in zucchini.
7. Pour out the batter in the paper-lined cupcake pan while filling two-third of each cupcake cup.
8. Put the pan in the preheated oven for 20 – 25 minutes or until cooked through.
9. Set it aside to cool for at least 10 minutes.
10. Meanwhile, prepare the brown butter frosting.
11. In a saucepan, put margarine, brown sugar and milk. Bring it to a boil.
12. Cook for 2 minutes on medium heat, while stirring constantly.
13. Remove the saucepan off the stove.
14. Stir in vanilla extract.
15. Set aside till it becomes lukewarm.
16. Slowly and gradually, add icing sugar in it while beating continuously. Beat till it becomes smooth and spreadable.
17. Spread it over the cupcakes and serve.

Colorful Cupcakes

Serving Size

    Makes 12 – 14 cupcakes

Nutritional Facts (Values per Cupcake)

    Calories/Cupcake: 347.5

    Protein: 3.6 g

    Total Fat: 15.5 g

    Cholesterol: 46.5 mg

    Total Carbohydrate: 49 g

Ingredients

    White cake mix – 19 ½ oz.

    Vegetable oil – 1/3 cup

    Eggs – 3

    Water – 1 cup

    Red food coloring – 2 Tbsp

    Pink food coloring – 2 Tbsp

    Yellow food coloring – 2 Tbsp

    Green food coloring – 2 Tbsp

    Blue food coloring – 2 Tbsp

    Purple food coloring – 2 Tbsp

    Cream cheese frosting – 8 oz.

Preparation Method

1. Set the oven to preheat at 350°F.
2. Line a cupcake baking pan with paper liners.

3. Make the cake batter using the white cake mix, egg, oil, as instructed on the cake mix box.

4. Divide the batter evenly into 6 different bowls.

5. Add each food coloring in each bowl. Mix well. Now you will have 6 different colored batters.

6. Pour 1 teaspoon of red colored batter in each of the paper-lined cups followed by one teaspoon of green colored batter, the another color and so on. Don't worry the batters won't mix with each other.

7. Put it in the preheated oven for 18 – 20 minutes or until a toothpick when inserted in it comes out clean.

8. Set aside to cool for at least 10 minutes.

9. Top up the cupcakes with cream cheese frosting and serve.

Lemon Flavored Yoghurt Cupcakes

Serving Size

Makes 12 cupcakes

Nutritional Facts (Values per Cupcake)

Calories/Cupcake: 193.4

Protein: 2.3 g

Total Fat: 8.5 g

Cholesterol: 37 mg

Total Carbohydrate: 27.5 g

Ingredients

Plain yogurt – half cup

Sugar – 1 cup

Flour – 1 ½ cups

Grated lemon zest – 1 tsp

Baking powder – 1 tsp

Melted unsalted butter – half cup

Lemon extract – ½ tsp

Egg – 1

Fresh lemon juice – 3 tbsp

Salt – ¼ tsp

Preparation Method

1. Set the oven to preheat at 350°F.
2. Line a muffin baking pan with paper liners.
3. Combine baking powder, flour and salt in a bowl. Mix well.

4. In another large bowl, combine butter, sugar and egg. Whisk till it becomes smooth.

5. Now add in it, lemon extract, lemon juice, yoghurt and grated lemon zest. Beat till it becomes smooth.

6. Fold the flour mixture in the batter.

7. Pour out the batter in the paper-lined muffin pan while filling ¾ of each muffin tin.

8. Put the pan in the preheated oven for 20 – 25 minutes or until the cupcakes spring back when lightly touched in the center.

9. Set aside to cool, for at least 10 minutes.

Freshly homemade Lemon Flavored Yoghurt Cupcakes are ready to devour.

Nutty German Cupcakes

Serving Size

Makes 18 cupcakes

Nutritional Facts (Values per Cupcake)

Calories/Cupcake: 346

Protein: 5.1 g

Total Fat: 17.7 g

Cholesterol: 48.3 mg

Total Carbohydrate: 50 g

Ingredients for Cupcake

Unsweetened Dutch cocoa powder – half cup

Melted unsalted butter – 6 Tbsp

Sugar – 1 ½ cups

Baking soda – ¾ tsp

Egg yolk – 1

All purpose flour – 1 ½ cups

Almond essence – ½ tsp

Baking powder – ¾ tsp

Whole milk – ¾ cup

Egg – 1

Hot water – ¾ cup

Salt – ¾ tsp

Ingredients for Coconut Filling

Chopped pecans – 1 cup

Sweetened coconut flakes – 7 oz.

Sweetened condensed milk – 14 oz.

Ingredients for Chocolate Icing

Full fat cream – half cup

Chocolate chips – 8 oz.

Preparation Method

To make the Coconut Filling,

1. Combine the chopped pecans and half of the coconut flakes in a baking sheet.
2. Put it in the oven for about 8 minutes or till the coconut becomes light brown.
3. Carefully, take the sheet out of the oven and pour out its contents in a bowl.
4. Stir in the remaining coconut flakes and condensed milk. Mix well and set aside.

To make the cupcakes,

5. Set the oven to preheat at 350°F.
6. Line a cupcake baking pan with paper liners.
7. Sift together the sugar, all purpose flour, baking soda, unsweetened Dutch cocoa powder, , as well as the baking powder and salt in a large bowl and mix well.
8. In another large bowl, combine milk, egg, butter, egg yolk, hot water and almond essence. Whisk well.
9. Fold the flour mixture in the egg mixture.
10. Pour out the batter in the paper-lined cupcakes while filling ¾ of each cupcake tin.
11. Spoon 1 – 2 tablespoons of the coconut filling on top of the batter.
12. Put the pan in the preheated oven for 15 – 18 minutes.
13. Set aside to cool for at least 10 minutes.
14. Meanwhile, mix the melted chocolate with cream to make the icing.
15. Spread the icing on the cupcakes with a spoon or you can also top it over the cupcakes through a piping bag.
16. Put it in the refrigerator for 10 minutes and serve.

Cheesilicious Cupcakes

Serving Size

Makes 9 cupcakes

Nutritional Facts (Values per Cupcake)

Calories/Cupcake: 173

Protein: 3.7 g

Total Fat: 7.9 g

Cholesterol: 42 mg

Total Carbohydrate: 22 g

Ingredients

All purpose flour, sifted – 1 cup

Velveeta cheese, grated – ¼ cup

Sugar – ¼ cup

Sweetened condensed milk – 4 oz.

Unsalted butter – ¼ cup

Cheddar cheese, grated – ¼ cup

Baking powder – 1 tsp

Orange essence – ¼ tsp

Egg – 1

Pinch of salt

Preparation Method

1. Set the oven to preheat at 350°F.
2. Line a muffin baking pan with paper liners.
3. Mix baking powder, flour and salt in a bowl. Set aside.
4. In another blow, combine sugar, butter, egg and orange essence. Beat well.

5. Fold the flour mixture and condensed milk in the egg batter, in the following manner:

One-third of flour mixture – half of condensed milk – one third of flour mixture – remaining condensed milk – remaining flour mixture.

6. Finally, add in the Velveeta cheese. Blend well.

7. Pour out the batter in the paper-lined muffin pan while filling ¾ of each muffin tin.

8. Top it up with grated cheddar cheese.

9. Put the pan in the preheated oven for 20 – 25 minutes or till cooked through.

10. The Cheesilicious Cupcakes are ready to devour.

Scented Cupcakes

Serving Size

Makes 12 cupcakes

Nutritional Facts (Values per Cupcake)

Calories/Cupcake: 223

Protein: 2.1 g

Total Fat: 12.2 g

Cholesterol: 57.7 mg

Total Carbohydrate: 26.6 g

Ingredients for Cupcakes

Free range eggs – 2

Margarine – 4 oz.

Self raising flour – 4 oz.

Powdered sugar – 4 oz.

Ingredients for Scented ingredients

Lemon rind – ½ tsp

Vanilla essence – ½ tsp

Orange rind – ½ tsp

Almond essence – ½ tsp

Rose essence – ½ tsp

Ingredients for Icing

Butter, softened – 2 oz.

Icing sugar – 4 oz.

Vanilla essence – 1 tsp

Crystallized Rose petals and lavender flowers to garnish

Preparation Method

1. Set the oven to preheat at 375°F.
2. Line a cupcake baking pan with paper liners.
3. In a large mixing bowl, combine margarine and sugar, Whisk till it becomes light and fluffy.
4. Beat the eggs separately.
5. Start adding the beaten eggs and sifted flour in the margarine mixture. Add both the ingredients alternatively, spoon by spoon. Do not add it all together. Keep whisking while you add flour and egg.
6. Add all the scented ingredients in this batter. Mix well. (You can add a little milk if you think the batter is very stiff).
7. Pour out the batter in the paper-lined cupcake pan while filling ¾ of each cupcake tin.
8. Put it in the preheated oven for 15 – 20 minutes or until cooked through.
9. Set aside to cool, for at least 10 minutes.
10. Meanwhile, beat together butter, icing sugar and vanilla essence to make the icing.
11. Spread the icing over the cupcakes.
12. Garnish each cupcake with a lavender flower and a crystallized rose petal.

Drunken Cupcakes with Butter Rum Frosting

Serving Size

    Makes 24 cupcakes

Nutritional Facts (Values per Cupcake)

    Calories/Cupcake: 398

    Protein: 2.7 g

    Total Fat: 19.4 g

    Cholesterol: 52.2 mg

    Total Carbohydrate: 48 g

Ingredients for Cupcakes

    Dark rum – half cup

    Butter recipe cake mix – 18 ½ oz.

    Vegetable oil – half cup

    Chopped pecans – 1 cup

    Eggs – 4

    Coconut flakes – half cup

    Vanilla instant pudding mix – 1 ¾ oz.

    Whole milk, cold – half cup

Ingredients for Butter Rum Frosting

    Dark rum – 4 Tbsp

    Icing sugar – 16 oz.

    Vanilla essence – 1 ½ tsp

    Butter, softened – half cup

Ingredients for Butter Rum Glaze

    Sugar – 1 cup

Unsalted butter – half cup

Dark rum – half cup

Preparation Method

To make the cupcakes,

1. Set the oven to preheat at 325°F.
2. Line a cupcake baking pan with paper liners.
3. In a nonstick pan, toast coconut flakes and chopped pecans for about 10 minutes while stirring occasionally.
4. In a large bowl, add all the remaining cupcake ingredients. Beat for 2 minutes with an electric beater on high speed.
5. Stir in the toasted pecans and coconut flakes. (Save one-third of it for garnishing).
6. Pour out the batter in the paper-lined cupcake pan while filling ¾ of each cupcake tin.
7. Put the pan in the preheated oven for 18 – 20 minutes or until a toothpick when inserted in it comes out clean.
8. Set aside to cool completely.

To make the butter rum glaze,

9. In a nonstick saucepan, melt butter.
10. Add in it, sugar and one-fourth cup of dark rum. Mix well.
11. Bring to mixture to a boil. Boil it for 5 minutes while stirring continuously.
12. Remove the saucepan off the heat.
13. Add in the remaining dark rum. Mix well.

To make the butter rum frosting,

14. Combine sugar, vanilla essence, butter and dark rum. Beat with an electric beater on medium speed till it becomes light and fluffy.
15. Dip the top of the each cupcake into the butter rum glaze.
16. Fill the butter rum frosting in a piping bag. Pipe it out on the cupcakes.

17. Sprinkle, if any glaze is left, over the top of frosting.
18. Garnish with the remaining toasted pecan-coconut flakes.

Diabetic Cupcakes

Serving Size

Makes 12 cupcakes

Nutritional Facts (Values per Cupcake)

Calories/Cupcake: 102

Protein: 2.7 g

Total Fat: 0.7 g

Cholesterol: 18 mg

Total Carbohydrate: 21.8 g

Ingredients

Natural unsweetened applesauce – half cup

Egg – 1

White flour – ¾ cup

Clove, crushed – ¼ tsp

White pepper – ½ tsp

Molasses – 2 tbsp

Cinnamon powder – ½ tsp

Whole wheat flour – ¾ cup

Baking soda – ½ tsp

Brown sugar – 1/3 cup

Ground ginger – 1 ¼ tsp

Buttermilk – ½ cup

Water – ¼ cup

Salt – ½ tsp

Cooking spray

Preparation Method

1. Set the oven to preheat at 350°F.

2. Grease a nonstick cupcake baking pan with cooking spray.

3. In a large bowl, combine white flour, whole wheat flour, ground ginger, white pepper, clove, cinnamon powder, baking soda and salt. Whisk well using a wire whisk.

4. In another bowl, combine brown sugar, applesauce, water, buttermilk, egg and molasses. Mix well.

5. Fold the flour mixture in the applesauce mixture.

6. Pour out the batter in the greased cupcake pan while filling ¾ of each cupcake slot.

7. Put the pan in the preheated oven for about 30 minutes or until cooked through.

Choco Banana Cupcakes

Serving Size

Makes 12 cupcakes

Nutritional Facts (Values per Cupcake)

Calories/Cupcake: 181

Protein: 2.6 g

Total Fat: 8.1 g

Cholesterol: 28 mg

Total Carbohydrate: 26 g

Ingredients

Chocolate chips – ½ cup

Ripe bananas, mashed – 2 cup

Buttermilk – ¼ cup

Butter, softened – ¼ cup

Baking powder – ¼ tsp

White sugar – ¼ cup

All purpose flour – 1 cup

Egg – 1

Packed brown sugar – ¼ cup

Cinnamon powder– ¼ tsp

Vanilla essence – ½ tsp

Baking soda – ¼ tsp

Brown sugar – 1 Tbsp

Chopped walnuts – ¼ cup

Salt– ¼ tsp

Preparation Method

1. Set the oven to preheat at 350°F.
2. Line a cupcake baking pan with paper liners.
3. In a bowl, sift together baking powder, flour, salt and baking soda. Mix well and set aside.
4. In a large bowl, combine butter, white sugar and packed brown sugars. Beat till it becomes light and fluffy.
5. Add mashed bananas in it. Beat for another minute.
6. Add egg in it and beat well.
7. Finally beat in vanilla essence.
8. Start adding the flour mixture and buttermilk in it. Add both the things alternatively, spoon by spoon. Do not add it all together. Keep beating while you add the flour mixture and buttermilk.
9. Beat till all the ingredients are thoroughly blended.
10. Add chocolate chips in it. Mix well.
11. Spoon out the batter in the paper-lined cupcake tray while filling ¾ of each cupcake tin.
12. In a small bowl, mix cinnamon powder, brown sugar and walnuts. Top it over the cupcakes.
13. Put the cupcake pan in the preheated oven for 20 – 22 minutes or until cooked through.
14. Let it cool for a while and then serve.

Tequila Cupcakes

Serving Size

Makes 12 cupcakes

Nutritional Facts (Values per Cupcake)

Calories/Cupcake: 297

Protein: 2.2 g

Total Fat: 8.8 g

Cholesterol: 0 mg

Total Carbohydrate: 53.5 g

Ingredients for Cupcakes

Tequila – 2 Tbsp

Baking powder – ½ tsp

Fresh lime juice – ¼ cup

Canola oil – ¼ cup

Vanilla essence – ½ tsp

Lime zest, grated – 1 ½ tsp

Baking soda – ¼ tsp

All purpose flour – 1 1/3 cup

Granulated sugar – ¾ cup

Soymilk – 1 cup

Salt – ½ tsp

Ingredients for Frosting

Icing sugar – 2 cups

Tequila – 1 Tbsp

Margarine – ¼ cup

Lime juice – 3 Tbsp

Green food coloring

Soymilk – 1 Tbsp

Pinch of kosher salt

Decorative sugar crystals – ½ cup

Preparation Method

1. Set the oven to preheat at 350°F.
2. Line a cupcake baking pan with paper liners.
3. In a bowl, combine lime juice, soy milk, lime zest, tequila, oil, sugar and vanilla essence. Beat well.
4. In another bowl, mix baking soda, flour, baking powder and salt.
5. Fold the flour mixture in the tequila mixture.
6. Pour out the batter in the liners while filling ¾ of each cupcake tin.
7. Put the pan in the preheated oven for 20 – 22 minutes or until a toothpick when inserted in it comes out clean.
8. Set aside. Allow it to cool completely.
9. Meanwhile, prepare the frosting.
10. In a large mixing bowl, blend margarine till it becomes light and fluffy.
11. Add soy milk, tequila, lime juice and a few drops of green food coloring in it. Mix well.
12. Now add icing sugar in it and blend till it becomes smooth and creamy.
13. Refrigerate till it achieves a spreadable consistency.
14. Spread the frosting on the cupcakes.
15. Roll out the outer edges of the cupcakes in decorative sugar crystals.

Cookies 'n' Cream Cupcakes

Serving Size

Makes 12 cupcakes

Nutritional Facts (Values per Cupcake)

Calories/Cupcake: 511

Protein: 3.2 g

Total Fat: 26.4 g

Cholesterol: 23.8 mg

Total Carbohydrate: 68 g

Ingredients for Cupcakes

10 Oreo cookies

All purpose flour – 1 cup

White sugar – ¾ cup

Baking powder – ½ tsp

Cocoa powder, unsweetened – 1/3 cup

Apple cider vinegar – 1 tsp

Baking soda – ¾ tsp

Almond extract – ½ tsp

Canola oil – 1/3 cup

Vanilla extract – 1 tsp

Milk – 1 cup

Salt – ¼ tsp

Ingredients for Oreo Frosting

5 Oreo cookies, coarsely chopped

Shortening – half cup

Milk – ¼ cup

Icing sugar – 3 ½ cups

Cup butter – half cup

Vanilla extract – 1 ½ tsp

12 whole Oreo cookies to garnish

Preparation Method

To make the cupcakes,

1. Set the oven to preheat at 350°F.
2. Line muffin cups with paper liners.
3. In a bowl, sift together cocoa powder, flour, baking powder, salt and baking soda. Mix well and set aside.
4. In another large bowl, combine milk and apple cider vinegar. Whisk and set aside till it starts to curdle.
5. Add in it vanilla extract, almond extract, oil and sugar. Beat with an electric beater, till it becomes foamy.
6. Add half of the flour mixture and beat well.
7. Add the remaining half and beat again. Beat till all the lumps are dissolved.
8. Coarsely chop the Oreo cookies and add them in the batter. Stir to mix.
9. Pour out the batter in the paper-lined muffin pan while filling ¾ of each muffin tin.
10. Put the pan in the preheated oven for 18 – 20 minutes or until a toothpick when inserted in it comes out clean.
11. Set aside to cool completely.

To make the Oreo frosting,

12. In a bowl, combine butter and shortening. Beat for 5 minutes with an electric beater on medium-high speed.
13. Reduce the speed of the beater to low and start adding sugar gradually. Keep on beating while you add sugar.

14. Once all the sugar is added, increase the speed of the beater to medium and beat for 3 more minutes.

15. Add in it the vanilla extract and milk. Beat for 5 more minutes or till it becomes fluffy.

16. Stir in the chopped Oreo cookies.

17. Spread the Oreo frosting over the cupcakes.

18. Stand a whole Oreo cookie on top of each cupcake and serve.

Blueberry Cupcakes

Serving Size

Makes 12 – 14 cupcakes

Nutritional Facts (Values per Cupcake)

Calories/Cupcake: 240

Protein: 3 g

Total Fat: 8.4 g

Cholesterol: 50.5 mg

Total Carbohydrate: 38.8 g

Ingredients

Fresh blueberries – 4 cups (approx. 400 grams)

Soft butter – 4 ½ oz.

Cinnamon powder – ¼ tsp

Milk – 5 cups

Icing sugar – 2 Tbsp

All purpose flour – 1 cup

White sugar – 1 ¼ cups

Baking powder -2 tsp

Eggs – 2

Cornstarch – 2 ½ Tbsp

Salt – ¼ tsp

Vanilla essence – 1 tsp

Preparation Method

1. Set the oven to preheat at 375°F.
2. Line a cupcake baking pan with paper liners.

3. In a bowl, mix corn starch, flour, salt, baking powder and cinnamon powder. Set aside.
4. In another large mixing bowl, combine butter and sugar. Beat till it becomes creamy.
5. Add one egg in it. Beat well.
6. Add another egg and vanilla essence. Beat till it becomes a smooth batter.
7. Fold half of the flour mixture in it.
8. Add milk and mix well.
9. Fold in the remaining flour mixture and blueberries. Mix well.
10. Spoon out the batter in the paper-lined cupcake pan while filling ¾ of each liner.
11. Sprinkle the icing sugar on top of it.
12. Put the pan in the preheated oven for 25 – 30 minutes on until cooked through.

Let it cool for a while and then serve.

Peanut Butter Treat

Serving Size

Makes 12 cupcakes

Nutritional Facts (Values per Cupcake)

Calories/Cupcake: 267

Protein: 6 g

Total Fat: 14.7 g

Cholesterol: 32.1 mg

Total Carbohydrate: 29.7 g

Ingredients

Creamy peanut butter – ¾ cup

Egg – 1

All purpose flour – 1 cup

Soft unsalted butter – 3 oz.

Brown sugar – 1 cup

Milk – ½ cup

Baking powder – 1 tsp

Vanilla essence – 1 tsp

Salt – ¼ tsp

Preparation Method

1. Set the oven to preheat at 350°F.
2. Line a cupcake baking pan with paper liners.
3. In a large bowl, sift together baking powder, flour and salt. Mix well and set aside.
4. In another large bowl, combine brown sugar, peanut butter and butter. Using an electric beater on medium speed, beat for about 60 seconds or till it becomes smooth.

5. Add egg and vanilla essence in it. Beat for another minute.

6. Reduce the speed of the beater to low. Start adding milk and the flour mixture in it, in the following manner:

One third flour mixture – half milk – One third flour mixture – remaining milk – remaining flour mixture. Keep on beating constantly while you add the flour mixture and milk.

7. Beat for a few minutes till no large lumps remain and it becomes a smooth mixture.

8. Pour out the batter in the liners while filling ¾ of each cupcake liner.

9. Put the pan in the preheated oven for 20 – 22 minutes or until a toothpick when inserted in it comes out clean.

Let it cool for a while and then serve.

Spicy Coconut Cupcakes with Orange Cheese Frosting

Serving Size

Makes 18 cupcakes

Nutritional Facts (Values per Cupcake)

Calories/Cupcake: 335

Protein: 3.3 g

Total Fat: 10.4 g

Cholesterol: 40.7 mg

Total Carbohydrate: 58.8 g

Ingredients for Cupcakes

Grand Marnier – 1 tsp

Unsalted butter – ½ cup

Fresh Orange zest – 3 Tbsp

Fresh orange Juice – ¼ cup

Ground nutmeg – ¼ tsp

Coconut flakes – ½ cup

Eggs – 2

Baking soda – 1 tsp

Ground cloves – ¼ tsp

Coconut milk – ½ cup

Cake flour – 2 ½ cups

Brown sugar – ½ cup

Cinnamon powder – 1 tsp

Buttermilk – ½ cup

Baking powder – 1 tsp

White sugar – 1 cup

Ground ginger – ½ tsp

Salt – 1 tsp

Ingredients for Orange Cheese Frosting

Cream cheese – 2 oz.

Coconut milk – 2 Tbsp

Fresh orange juice – 2 Tbsp

Grand Marnier – ½ tsp

Icing sugar – 4 cups

Preparation Method

1. Set the oven to preheat at 350°F.
2. Put paper liners in 18 cupcake tins.
3. In a bowl, combine flour, salt, baking soda, cinnamon powder, baking powder, ginger, cloves and nutmeg. Whisk well and set aside.
4. In another large bowl, blend butter till it becomes light and fluffy.
5. Add eggs, white sugar and brown sugar in it. Beat for about 5 minutes or till it becomes fluffy.
6. Add the Grand Marnier in it and beat for another minute.
7. Add orange juice and one-third of the flour mixture. Beat till all the ingredients are thoroughly blended.
8. Now add the coconut milk and half of the remaining flour mixture. Beat again for a minute.
9. Finally add the remaining flour mixture and buttermilk. Beat till all the ingredients are thoroughly blended.
10. Stir in orange zest and coconut flakes.
11. Pour out the batter in the liners while filling ¾ of each cupcake tin.
12. Put the pan in the preheated oven for 18 – 20 minutes or until a toothpick when inserted in it comes out clean.

13. Set aside to cool for at least 15 minutes.
14. To make the frosting,
15. In a bowl, beat the cream cheese till it becomes smooth and creamy.
16. Add orange juice and icing sugar in it. Beat till it becomes smooth.
17. Finally add the Grand Marnier and coconut milk in it. Beat till it achieves a spreadable consistency.
18. Frost the cupcakes and serve.

Brown Orange Cupcakes

Serving Size

Makes 12 cupcakes

Nutritional Facts (Values per Cupcake)

Calories/Cupcake: 368

Protein: 3.3 g

Total Fat: 20.3 g

Cholesterol: 82.2 mg

Total Carbohydrate: 45 g

Ingredients for Cupcakes

Buttermilk – ½ cup

Dutch cocoa powder – 3 Tbsp

Eggs – 2

Baking powder – ½ tsp

Unsalted butter, melted – ¼ cup

Sugar – ¾ cup

Hot water – ¼ cup

Baking soda – ½ tsp

Fresh orange zest, grated – 2 Tbsp

All purpose flour – 1 ¼ cups

Salt – ¼ tsp

Vanilla essence – ½ tsp

Ingredients for Frosting

Unsalted butter – 1 cup

Bittersweet chocolate, melted – 6 oz.

Icing sugar – 2 cup

Preparation Method

1. Set the oven to preheat at 350°F.
2. Line a cupcake baking pan with paper liners.
3. In a small bowl, dissolve Dutch cocoa powder into hot water. Set aside.
4. In another bowl, combine baking soda, baking powder, flour and salt. Mix well and set aside.
5. In another large bowl, combine eggs and sugar. Whisk well.
6. Add in it vanilla essence and butter milk. Whisk well.
7. Whisk in the dissolved cocoa powder.
8. Add melted butter in it. Whisk again to mix all the ingredients
9. Fold the flour mixture in it.
10. Pour out the batter in the paper-lined cupcake pan while filling ¾ of each cupcake tin.
11. Put the pan in the preheated oven for 15 – 20 minutes or until a toothpick when inserted in it comes out clean.
12. Set aside to cool for at least 15 minutes.
13. To make the frosting,
14. Beat together butter and icing sugar till it becomes smooth.
15. Add melted chocolate in it and beat for another 2 – 3 minutes.
16. Pour out the frosting in a pastry bag.
17. Beat in the melted chocolate until combined.
18. Pipe a spiral of frosting on top of each cupcake.
19. Put the cupcakes in the refrigerator for 10 minutes and then serve.

Coconut Cupcakes with Condensed Milk Frosting

Serving Size

Makes 14 cupcakes

Nutritional Facts (Values per Cupcake)

Calories/Cupcake: 594

Protein: 7.2 g

Total Fat: 31 g

Cholesterol: 128 mg

Total Carbohydrate: 73.8 g

Ingredients for Cupcakes

Buttermilk – ¾ cup

Shortening – ¼ cup

Sweetened condensed milk – ½ cup

Egg yolks – 3

Sugar – 1 cup

Coconut milk – ½ cup

Vanilla essence – ½ tsp

Unsalted butter – ½ cup

Evaporated milk

All-purpose flour– 1 cup

Egg whites – 3

Baking soda – ½ tsp

Salt – ½ tsp

Toasted coconut flakes – 1 cup

Ingredients for Condensed Milk Frosting

Condensed Milk Frosting

Unsalted butter – 7 oz.

Sweetened condensed milk – 1 ¾ cup

Vanilla essence – 1 tsp

Cornstarch – 3 Tbsp

Egg yolks – 2

Salt – ¼ tsp

Sugar – ¾ cup

Icing sugar – 1 cup

Water – ¼ cup

Preparation Method

1. Set the oven to preheat at 350°F.
2. Line a cupcake baking pan with paper liners.
3. In a bowl, combine salt, flour and baking soda. Mix well and set aside.
4. In another large bowl, combine butter, shortening and sugar. Using an electric beat on medium speed, beat till it becomes light and fluffy.
5. Beat in the egg yolks, one at a time. Keep on beating till the yellow color of yolks disappears.
6. Beat in the vanilla essence.
7. Reduce the speed of the beater to low. Start adding buttermilk and the flour mixture in it, in the following manner:

One third flour mixture – half buttermilk – One third flour mixture – remaining buttermilk – remaining flour mixture. Keep on beating constantly while you are adding the flour mixture and buttermilk.

8. Beat the egg whites separately in a small bowl till it becomes stiff.
9. Fold the beaten egg whites into the cake batter.
10. Pour out the batter in the paper-lined cupcake pan while filling ¾ of each cupcake tin.

11. Put the pan in the preheated oven for 20 – 25 minutes or until a toothpick when inserted in it comes out clean.

12. Meanwhile, mix the sweetened condensed milk, evaporated milk and coconut milk in a large bowl.

13. Fill a meat injector with this milk mixture.

14. When the cupcakes are cooked through, set them aside to cool.

15. While the cupcakes are still warm, inject about half ounce of the sweet milk mixture into each cupcake. You can inject altogether in the center of the cupcake or in 2 – 3 different spots.

16. Put the cupcakes in the refrigerator for at least 2 hours.

To make the condensed milk frosting,

17. Set the oven to preheat at 425°F.

18. Put the sweetened condensed milk in a pie plate and cover it with aluminum foil.

19. Place the plate in a large saucepan. Make sure the plate sits flat and straight.

20. Pour hot water into the saucepan halfway up to the pie plate.

21. Put the saucepan in the preheated oven for 75 minutes.

22. Carefully take it out of the oven and set aside to cool. Stir the condensed milk.

23. Meanwhile, combine sugar, salt and cornstarch in a small saucepan.

24. Stir in water then whisk in the condensed milk that you just heated and cooled.

25. Bring it to a boil over medium heat. Boil for a minute while whisking continuously.

26. Remove the saucepan off heat.

27. Beat the egg yolks in a separate bowl.

28. Gradually, add the condensed milk mixture into the egg yolks while whisking constantly.

29. Whisk in the vanilla essence.

30. Pass the mixture through a wire strainer. Discard the residue and set aside the liquid to cool completely.

31. In a large mixing bowl, beat butter till it becomes light and fluffy.

32. Beat in it the cooled condensed milk mixture.

33. Beat in the icing sugar. Keep on beating till it achieves a spreadable consistency.

34. Spread this frosting over each cupcake.

35. Drizzle with toasted coconut flakes and serve.

Death by Chocolate Cupcakes

Serving Size

Makes 12 cupcakes

Nutritional Facts (Values per Cupcake)

Calories/Cupcake: 115

Protein: 1.9 g

Total Fat: 9.6 g

Cholesterol: 42 mg

Total Carbohydrate: 6.9 g

Ingredients

Hot water – 1 Tbsp

Egg – 1

All purpose flour – ¼ cup

Icing sugar – 2 Tbsp

Butter, melted – 1 Tbsp

Cocoa powder – 1 tsp

Dark chocolate, grated – 1/3 cup

Self raising flour – 2 Tbsp

Drinking chocolate – 1 tsp

Instant coffee powder – 1 tsp

Full fat cream – 1 cup

Cocoa powder to garnish

Preparation Method

1. Set the oven to preheat at 350°F.
2. Line a cupcake baking pan with paper liners.

3. In a bowl, sift together both the flours. Mix well and set aside.

4. In a large mixing bowl, dissolve coffee in hot water.

5. Add melted butter in it. Mix well.

6. Add egg and sugar in it. Using an electric beater, beat till it becomes thick.

7. Fold the flour mixture.

8. Fold in the coffee mixture and grated chocolate in it.

9. Pour out the batter in the paper-lined cupcake pan while filling ¾ of each liner.

10. Put the pan in the preheated oven for 15 – 18 minutes or until a toothpick when inserted in it comes out clean.

11. Set is aside to cool for at least 10 minutes.

12. Meanwhile, beat the cream till it becomes thick.

13. Mix cocoa powder and drinking chocolate in a separate bowl and then fold in the cream.

14. Spoon over the mixture on top of each cupcake.

15. Sprinkle a bit of cocoa powder and serve.

Berrylicious White Chocolate Cupcakes

Serving Size

Makes 14 cupcakes

Nutritional Facts (Values per Cupcake)

Calories/Cupcake: 209

Protein: 3.5 g

Total Fat: 8.8 g

Cholesterol: 17.2 mg

Total Carbohydrate: 29.5 g

Ingredients

White chocolate, grated – 4 oz.

All purpose flour – 10 oz.

Canola oil – 5 Tbsp

Cinnamon powder – ½ tsp

Baking powder – 3 tsp

Milk – 1 cup

Sugar – 7 tbsp

Ground nutmeg – ½ tsp

Cranberries – 1 cup

Egg – 1

Preparation Method

1. Set the oven to preheat at 350°F.
2. Line a cupcake baking pan with paper liners.
3. In a large bowl, combine baking powder, flour, white chocolate, nutmeg and cinnamon powder. Mix well and set aside.

4. In another bowl, beat egg.

5. Beat in sugar, milk and oil. Beat till all the ingredients are thoroughly blended.

6. Fold the flour mixture in it.

7. Stir in cranberries. Blend for just another minute.

8. Pour out the batter in the paper-lined cupcake pan while filling ¾ of each cupcake tin.

9. Put the pan in the preheated oven for 18 – 20 minutes or until cooked through.

Mocha Cupcakes

Serving Size

Makes 18 cupcakes

Nutritional Facts (Values per Cupcake)

Calories/Cupcake: 273

Protein: 3.1 g

Total Fat: 9.6 g

Cholesterol: 43.2 mg

Total Carbohydrate: 44.4 g

Ingredients for Cupcakes

Eggs – 2

All purpose flour – 2 cups

Dutch processed cocoa powder – ½ cup

Butter – ½ cup

Baking soda – at least 1 tsp

Sugar – 1 cup

Boiling water – 1 cup

Vanilla essence – 1 tsp

Salt – ½ tsp

Ingredients for Mocha Frosting

Cocoa powder – ½ cup

Vanilla essence – ½ tsp

Icing sugar – 3 cups

Unsalted butter, softened – 1/3 cup

Cold strong black coffee – as required

Pinch of salt

Preparation Method

To make the cupcakes,

1. Set the oven to preheat at 350°F.
2. Line a cupcake baking pan with paper liners.
3. In a small bowl, dissolve Dutch processed cocoa powder in boiling water. Set aside.
4. In another small bowl, sift together baking soda, flour and salt. Mix well and set aside.
5. In a large mixing bowl, beat butter and sugar till it becomes soft and fluffy.
6. In medium bowl, cream butter and sugar with an electric mixer until fluffy.
7. Add one egg and beat well.
8. Beat in another egg.
9. Add the Dutch processed cocoa mixture in it. Mix well.
10. Stir in vanilla essence.
11. Fold in the flour mixture.
12. Pour out the batter in the paper-lined cupcake pan while filling ¾ of each cupcake tin.
13. Put the pan in the preheated oven for 15 – 20 minutes or until a toothpick when inserted in it comes out clean.
14. Set aside to cool. Meanwhile, make the mocha frosting.

To make the mocha frosting,

15. Sift together sugar and cocoa powder. Mix well.
16. In a large mixing bowl, beat butter till it becomes smooth.
17. Beat in salt and vanilla essence.
18. Beat in the sugar-cocoa mixture.

19. Beat in the cold coffee. Keep adding and beating till it achieves a spreadable consistency. Don't put too much coffee or it will thin out the frosting.

20. Frost the cupcakes and serve.

Celebration Cupcakes

Serving Size

Makes 22 cupcakes

Nutritional Facts (Values per Cupcake)

Calories/Cupcake: 288

Protein: 2.7 g

Total Fat: 18.2 g

Cholesterol: 54.5 mg

Total Carbohydrate: 25.7 g

Ingredients for Cupcakes

Vodka – ¼ cup

Vanilla instant pudding mix – 3 ½ oz.

Whole milk – ¾ cup

Yellow cake mix – 18 ¼ oz.

Eggs – 4

Vegetable oil – 1 cup

Kahlua – ¼ cup plus another 2 tablespoons Kahlua

Vanilla extract – 1 tsp

Ingredients for Frosting

Kahlua – 1 Tbsp

Icing sugar – 2 Tbsp

Full fat cream – 1 cup

Semisweet chocolate shavings – 2 Tbsp

Preparation Method

1. Set the oven to preheat at 350°F.

2. Place paper liners in a cupcake baking pan.

3. In a large mixing bowl, combine yellow cake mix, vanilla instant pudding mix, milk, oil, vodka, vanilla extract and ¼ cup of Kahlua.

4. Using an electric mixer on low speed, blend it for 30 seconds. Increase the increase of the beater to high and beat for 2 more minutes. Scrape down the sides of the bowl.

5. Pour out the batter in the paper-lined cupcake pan while filling ¾ of each liner.

6. Put it in the preheated oven for 18 – 20 minutes or till the cupcakes spring back when lightly pressed in the center.

7. Set aside to cool for 5 minutes.

8. Brush 2 tablespoons Kahlua on top of the cupcakes.

To make the frosting,

9. In a large mixing bowl, beat cream with an electric beater on high speed. Beat for about 2 minutes or till the cream thickens.

10. Turn off the beater and add sugar and one tablespoon Kahlua.

11. Start the beater again on high speed and beat for 2 more minutes,

12. Pour a spoonful of this topping on each cupcake.

13. Garnish with chocolate shavings and serve.

Strawberry Marmalade Cupcakes

Serving Size

Makes 18 cupcakes

Nutritional Facts (Values per Cupcake)

Calories/Cupcake: 197

Protein: 2.8 g

Total Fat: 6.1 g

Cholesterol: 44.8 mg

Total Carbohydrate: 33.9 g

Ingredients

Strawberry marmalade – 1 cup

Buttermilk – ½ cup

Baking soda – ½ tsp

Eggs – 3

Baking powder – ½ tsp

Sugar – 1 cup

All purpose flour – 2 cups

Margarine – ½ cup

Salt – ¼ tsp

Preparation Method

1. Set the oven to preheat at 350°F.
2. Line a muffin baking pan with paper liners.
3. In a bowl, sift together baking powder, salt, baking soda and all-purpose flour. Mix well and set aside.
4. In another large bowl, beat sugar margarine and butter with an electric beater on medium speed. Beat for about 5 minutes or till it becomes light and creamy.

5. Start adding eggs in it. Add one egg at a time while beating constantly.

6. Add marmalade in it. Beat well.

7. Reduce the speed of the electric beater to low. Start adding the flour mixture and buttermilk in the following manner:

One third flour mixture – half buttermilk – One third flour mixture – remaining buttermilk – remaining flour mixture. Keep on beating constantly while you add the flour mixture and buttermilk.

8. Beat for a few minutes till no large lumps remain and it becomes a smooth mixture.

9. Pour out the batter in the paper-lined muffin pan while filling ¾ of each muffin tin.

10. Put the pan in the preheated oven for 20 – 25 minutes or until a toothpick when inserted in it comes out clean.

11. Let it cool for a while and then serve.

German Peppermint Cupcakes

Serving Size

Makes 24 cupcakes

Nutritional Facts (Values per Cupcake)

Calories/Cupcake: 311

Protein: 3.1 g

Total Fat: 16.4 g

Cholesterol: 39.3 mg

Total Carbohydrate: 40.5 g

Ingredients for Cupcakes

Sour cream – 1 cup

Eggs – 3

German chocolate cake mix – 18 ¼ oz.

Vegetable oil – ½ cup

Vanilla instant pudding mix – 3 ½ oz.

Semisweet chocolate chips – 1 cup

Water – ½ cup

Red food coloring – 2 Tbsp

Ingredients for Frosting

Cream cheese – 6 oz.

Peppermint extract – 1 tsp

White chocolate, melted and cooled – 6 oz.

Icing sugar – 2 cups

Butter – 4 Tbsp

Peppermint candies, crushed – 6

Preparation Method

1. Set the oven to preheat at 350°F.

2. Line a cupcake baking pan with paper liners.

3. In a large mixing bowl, put Vanilla instant pudding mix, German chocolate cake mix, water, sour cream, oil, eggs and red food coloring.

4. Using an electric mixer on low speed, blend it for 30 seconds. Increase the increase of the beater to high and beat for 2 more minutes. Scrape down the sides of the bowl.

5. Fold in the chocolate chips.

6. Pour out the batter in the paper-lined cupcake pan while filling ¾ of each cupcake tin.

7. Put the pan in the preheated oven for 18 – 20 minutes or until the cupcake spring back when lightly pressed in the center.

8. Set aside to cool for 15 minutes.

To make the frosting,

9. In a large mixing bowl, blend cream cheese and butter with an electric beater on low speed. Beat for 30 seconds.

10. Add melted and cooled white chocolate and beat for another 30 seconds.

11. Add in it the peppermint extract and sugar. Beat on low speed for 30 seconds then on medium speed till it achieves a spreadable consistency.

12. Frost the cupcakes.

13. Sprinkle the crushed peppermint candies on top of the frosting.

14. Put them in the refrigerator for 20 minutes.

Enjoy!

Mayonnaise in a Cupcake

Serving Size

    Makes 12 cupcakes

Nutritional Facts (Values per Cupcake)

    Calories/Cupcake: 398

    Protein: 5.7 g

    Total Fat: 21.2 g

    Cholesterol: 62 mg

    Total Carbohydrate: 52.1 g

Ingredients

    Mayonnaise – 1 cup

    Chocolate cake mix – 18 ¼ oz.

    Cinnamon powder – 1 tsp

    Water – 1 cup

    Chocolate chips – ¾ cup

    Eggs – 3

    Cooking spray to grease

Preparation Method

1. Set the oven to preheat at 350°F.
2. Lightly grease the muffin tins of a muffin baking pan.
3. In a large mixing bowl, combine mayonnaise, chocolate cake mix, eggs, water and cinnamon powder. Beat for 2 minutes with an electric beater on medium speed.
4. Pour out the batter in the greased muffin pan while filling ¾ of each muffin tin.
5. Put the pan in the preheated oven for 25 – 30 minutes or until cooked through.
6. Drizzle with chocolate chips.

7. Set aside to cool for 10 minutes and serve.

Boston Cream Surprise Cupcakes

Serving Size

Makes 20 cupcakes

Nutritional Facts (Values per Cupcake)

Calories/Cupcake: 350

Protein: 4 g

Total Fat: 23.5 g

Cholesterol: 128.4 mg

Total Carbohydrate: 31.7 g

Ingredients for cupcakes

Buttermilk – 1 cup

All purpose flour – 2 cups

Unsalted butter – ¾ cup

Eggs – 3

Salt – ¼ tsp

Sugar – 1 ½ cups

Cornstarch – 1 Tbsp

Vanilla essence – 1 tsp

Baking powder – 1 ½ tsp

Baking soda – ½ tsp

Ingredients for Cream Filling

Full fat cream, whipped – 1 cup

Milk – 1 cup

Cornstarch – 2 Tbsp

Egg yolks – 3

Vanilla essence – 1 tsp

Sugar – 1/3 cup

Unsalted butter – ½ cup

Ingredients for Chocolate glaze

Unsalted butter – 2 Tbsp

Corn syrup – 1 Tbsp

Full fat cream – 1 cup

Bittersweet chocolate, chopped – 8 oz.

Preparation Method

1. Set the oven to preheat at 350°F.
2. Line a muffin baking pan with paper liners.
3. In a bowl, sift together flour, cornstarch, baking powder, baking soda and salt. Mix well and set to the side.
4. In a large mixing bowl, beat butter and sugar with an electric beater on medium speed.
5. Beat in eggs and vanilla essence.
6. Reduce the speed of the electric beater to low. Start adding the flour mixture and buttermilk in the following manner:

One third flour mixture – half buttermilk – One third flour mixture – remaining buttermilk – remaining flour mixture. Keep on beating constantly while you add the flour mixture and buttermilk.

7. Beat for a few minutes till no large lumps remain and it becomes a smooth mixture.
8. Pour out the batter in the paper-lined muffin pan while filling ¾ of each muffin tin.
9. Put the pan in the preheated oven for 15 – 20 minutes or until cooked through.

Meanwhile make the cream filling. To make the cream filling,

10. In a bowl, whisk together sugar, egg yolks and cornstarch.
11. Boil milk in a medium saucepan and pour in the egg mixture. Whisk well.

12. Return the mixture to the saucepan over low heat. Keep on whisking constantly till the mixture thickens.

13. Pour it out into a bowl and whisk vanilla in it.

14. Whisk in butter, 1 tablespoon at a time. Keep on whisking till it becomes smooth.

15. Cover the bowl with plastic wrap and put it in the refrigerator.

16. When it is completely chilled, fold in whipped cream.

To make the chocolate glaze,

17. Combine cream and corn syrup in a saucepan. Bring it to a boil.

18. Put the chopped chocolate in a bowl and pour the hot cream–corn syrup mixture over it.

19. Let it sit for 5 minutes.

20. Stir to dissolve the chocolate.

21. Stir in butter.

To make the Boston cream surprise cupcakes,

22. Fill a pastry bag with cream filling. Pipe out a spiral of cream filling on top of each cupcake.

23. Drizzle with the chocolate glaze and serve.

Sweet Bacon Cupcakes

Serving Size

Makes 12 cupcakes

Nutritional Facts (Values per Cupcake)

Calories/Cupcake: 302

Protein: 4.7 g

Total Fat: 13.8 g

Cholesterol: 60.4 mg

Total Carbohydrate: 40.2 g

Ingredients for Cupcakes

Self rising flour – 2 ½ cups

Cooked minced bacon, drained – ½ cup

Butter – 4 ½ oz.

Brown sugar – 10 Tbsp

Baking soda – 2 tsp

Bacon drippings – 1 Tbsp

Maple syrup – 8 Tbsp

Eggs – 2

Baking powder – 1 tsp

Milk – ½ cup

Pinch of kosher salt

Ingredients for Maple Frosting

Maple syrup – 4 Tbsp

Butter – 8 Tbsp

Pinch of sea salt

Icing sugar – 2 cups

Preparation Method

1. Set the oven to preheat at 350°F.
2. Line a cupcake baking pan with paper liners.
3. In a bowl, sift together salt, flour, baking soda and baking powder. Mix well and set aside.
4. In a large mixing bowl, beat butter and bacon drippings till it becomes light and creamy.
5. Beat in brown sugar and maple syrup. Beat till all the ingredients are thoroughly blended.
6. Beat in eggs, one at a time.
7. Start adding the flour mixture and milk in the following manner:

One third flour mixture – half milk – One third flour mixture – remaining milk – remaining flour mixture. Keep on beating constantly while you add the flour mixture and milk.

8. Beat for a few minutes till no large lumps remain and it becomes a smooth mixture.
9. Fold in the cooked minced bacon.
10. Spoon out the batter in the paper-lined cupcake pan while filling ¾ of each cupcake tin.
11. Put the pan in the preheated oven for 18 – 22 minutes or until a toothpick when inserted in it comes out clean.
12. Set aside to cool for at least 10 minutes.

To make the maple frosting,

13. Beat together butter and maple syrup.
14. Beat in icing sugar, one tablespoon at time while beating constantly.
15. Stir in sea salt.
16. Frost the cupcakes and serve.

Divine Malt Cupcakes

Serving Size

Makes 18 cupcakes

Nutritional Facts (Values per Cupcake)

Calories/Cupcake: 514

Protein: 4 g

Total Fat: 28.8 g

Cholesterol: 70 mg

Total Carbohydrate: 63 g

Ingredients for Cupcakes

Whole milk – 2/3 cup

All purpose flour – 1 ½ cups

Espresso powder – ½ tsp

Baking powder – 1 tsp

Sour cream – 2/3 cup

Sugar – 1/3 cup

Salt – ½ tsp

Eggs – 2

Cocoa powder, unsweetened – half cup

Instant malted milk powder – 2/3 cup

Baking soda – 1 tsp

Canola oil – 2/3 cup

Chocolate chips – half cup

Vanilla extract – 1 tsp

Ingredients for Buttercream Frosting

Unsalted butter, softened – 1 ½ cups

Icing sugar – 4 ½ cups

Whipped cream – 4 Tbsp

Vanilla extract – 1 tsp

Tart cherry preserves – 2/3 cup

Preparation Method

To make the cupcakes,

1. Set the oven to preheat at 350°F.
2. Line a cupcake baking pan with paper liners.
3. In a bowl, sift together cocoa powder, flour, sugar, baking soda, salt and baking powder. Mix well and set aside.
4. In another large bowl, combine milk, espresso powder and malted milk powder. Beat well.
5. Beat in oil and eggs.
6. Fold the flour mixture in the egg mixture.
7. Beat in sour cream and vanilla extract.
8. Stir in the chocolate chips.
9. Pour out the batter in the paper-lined cupcake pan while filling ¾ of each cupcake tin.
10. Put the pan in the preheated oven for 18 – 20 minutes or until a toothpick when inserted in it comes out clean.
11. Set aside to cool for at least 10 minutes.

To make the buttercream frosting,

12. In a large mixing bowl, combine sugar and butter. Beat with an electric beater on medium speed, till it becomes smooth.
13. Beat in vanilla and whipped cream. Keep on beating till a spreadable consistency is achieved.
14. Beat in the tart cherry preserves.

15. Fill a pastry bag with this frosting.

16. Pipe a spiral out of it on each cupcake.

Enjoy!

Classic Sweet Potato Muffins

Serving Size

Makes 24 cupcakes

Nutritional Facts (Values per Cupcake)

Calories/Cupcake: 728

Protein: 4.6 g

Total Fat: 32 g

Cholesterol: 87 mg

Total Carbohydrate: 109 g

Ingredients

Sugar – 1 ½ cups

All-purpose flour – 2 cups

Canned sweet potatoes, mashed – 17 ¼ oz.

Eggs – 3

Baking soda – ½ tsp

Baking powder – 2 tsp

Butter, softened – 1 cup

Cinnamon powder – 1 tsp

Salt – ¼ tsp

Vanilla essence – ½ tsp

Preparation Method

1. Set the oven to preheat at 350°F.

2. Line a muffin baking pan with paper liners.

3. In a large bowl, sift together baking powder, flour, baking soda, salt and cinnamon powder. Mix well and set aside.

4. In another large mixing bowl, beat butter for 30 seconds, with an electric beater on medium speed.

5. Reduce the speed to low and beat in sugar. Keep on beating till it becomes light and fluffy.

6. Beat in eggs, one at a time while beating constantly on low speed.

7. Beat in sweet potatoes and vanilla essence. Beat till the batter thickens.

8. Pour out the batter in the paper-lined muffin pan while filling ¾ of each muffin tin.

9. Put the pan in the preheated oven for 18 – 20 minutes or until cooked through.

10. Set aside to cool for a while and then serve.

Simple Champagne Cupcakes

Serving Size

Makes 18 cupcakes

Nutritional Facts (Values per Cupcake)

Calories/Cupcake: 208

Protein: 3.2 g

Total Fat: 7 g

Cholesterol: 18 mg

Total Carbohydrate: 32 g

Ingredients

Egg whites – 6

Butter – 2/3 cup

Baking powder – 3 tsp

Sugar – 1 ½ cups

Champagne – ¾ cup

Flour – 2 ¾ cups

Salt – 1 tsp

Preparation Method

1. Set the oven to preheat at 350°F.
2. Line a cupcake baking pan with paper liners.
3. In a bowl, sift together flour, salt and baking powder. Mix well and set aside.
4. In another bowl, beat together sugar and butter till it becomes light and fluffy.
5. Start adding the flour mixture and champagne in the following manner:
6. One third flour mixture – half champagne – One third flour mixture – remaining champagne – remaining flour mixture. Keep on beating constantly while you add the flour mixture and champagne.

7. In another large bowl, beat the egg whites till it becomes stiff. Fold it in the batter.

8. Pour out the batter in the paper-lined cupcake pan while filling ¾ of each cupcake tin.

9. Put the pan in the preheated oven for 18 – 20 minutes or until cooked through.

Pineapple 'n' Coconut Cupcake

Serving Size

Makes 24 cupcakes

Nutritional Facts (Values per Cupcake)

Calories/Cupcake: 209

Protein: 1.8 g

Total Fat: 9.3 g

Cholesterol: 23.2 mg

Total Carbohydrate: 28.5 g

Ingredients

Rum extract – 1 tsp

Super moist cake mix – 18 ¼ oz.

Whipped vanilla frosting – 12 oz.

Canned crushed pineapple with juice – 8 oz.

Eggs – 3

Vegetable oil – 1/3 cup

Coconut extract – 1 tsp

Water – ¼ cup

Coconut flakes, sweetened – ¾ cup

Preparation Method

1. Set the oven to preheat at 375°F.

2. Line a cupcake baking pan with paper liners.

3. In a large mixing bowl, combine super moist cake mix, vegetable oil, water, eggs, coconut extract and canned crushed pineapple with juice. Beat on low speed for 30 seconds and then on medium speed for 2 minutes.

4. Pour out the batter in the paper-lined cupcake pan while filling ¾ of each cupcake tin.

5. Put the pan in the preheated oven for 18 – 22 minutes or until a toothpick when inserted in it comes out clean.

6. Set aside to cool for 10 minutes.

7. Meanwhile, mix the coconut extract, rum extract and whipped vanilla frosting to make the frosting.

8. Frost the cupcakes.

9. Drizzle with coconut flakes and serve.

Printed in Great Britain
by Amazon